Cliff
Richard

This diary belongs to...

Name:
....

Address:
....

....

....

Postcode:
....

Telephone:
....

Work:
....

Mobile:
....

Fax:
....

E-mail:
....

In an emergency...

Name:
....

Address:
....

....

....

Postcode:
....

Telephone:
....

Work:
....

Mobile:
....

Contact numbers

Name:

Tel:

Name:

Tel:

Name:

Tel:

Name:

Tel:

Name:

Tel:

Name:

Tel:

Name:

Tel:

Name:

Tel:

Name:

Tel:

Name:

Tel:

Contact numbers

Name:

Tel:

Name:

Tel:

Name:

Tel:

Name:

Tel:

Name:

Tel:

Name:

Tel:

Name:

Tel:

Name:

Tel:

Name:

Tel:

Name:

Tel:

Name:

Tel:

Contact numbers

Name:

Tel:

Name:

Tel:

Name:

Tel:

Name:

Tel:

Name:

Tel:

Name:

Tel:

Name:

Tel:

Name:

Tel:

Name:

Tel:

Name:

Tel:

Name:

Tel:

Conversions

1 in = 2.54 cm	1 in^2 = 6.4516 cm^2
1 cm = 0.3937 in	1 cm^2 = 0.155 in^2
1 ft = 0.3048 m	1 ft^2 = 0.0929 m^2
1 m = 3.2808 ft	1 m^2 = 10.7639 ft^2
1 yd = 0.9144 m	1 mile^2 = 2.59 km^2
1 m = 1.0936 yd	1 km^2 = 0.3861 miles^2
1 mile = 1.6093 km	1 acre = 0.4047 ha
1 km = 0.6214 miles	1 ha = 2.471 acres
1 in^3 = 16.387 cm^3	1 UK gal = 4.546 l
1 cm^3 = 0.06102 in^3	1 l = 0.22 UK gal
1 ft^3 = 0.02832 m^3	1 oz = 28.3495 g
1 m^3 = 35.3147 ft^3	1 g = 0.03527 oz
1 yd^3 = 0.76456 m^3	1 lb = 453.59 g
1 m^3 = 1.30795 yd^3	1 g = 0.002205 lb
1 US gal = 3.7854 l	1 kg = 2.2046 lb
1 l = 0.2642 US gal	1 t (long) = 1016.0469 kg
1 US gal = 0.8327 UK gal	1 kg = 0.00098 t (long)

Useful Websites

AA	www.theaa.com
RAC	www.rac.co.uk
Green Flag	www.greenflag.com
Eurotunnel	www.eurotunnel.com
Eurostar	www.eurostar.com
London Travel Info	www.tfl.gov.uk
National Rail	www.nationalrail.co.uk
National Express Coaches	www.nationalexpress.com
British Airways	www.britishairways.com
Virgin	www.virgin-atlantic.com
Flybe	www.flybe.com
EasyJet	www.easyjet.com
Ryanair	www.ryanair.com
Avis	www.avis.co.uk
Europcar	www.europcar.co.uk
Hertz	www.hertz.co.uk
UK Traffic Info	www.highways.gov.uk
Road Maps (Worldwide)	www.bing.com/maps
Road Maps (UK)	www.streetmap.co.uk
World Time Zones	www.worldtimezone.com

Useful Contacts

Tourist Information:
www.visitbritain.com
Telephone: 020 7578 1000

Healthcare:
www.nhs.uk
Telephone: 111 (non-emergency calls)
Telephone: 999 (emergency calls)

Police:
www.police.uk
Telephone: 101 (non-emergency calls)
Telephone: 999 (emergency calls)

Government Services:
www.gov.uk

Doctor:

Dentist:

Hospital:

Local Police Station:

Local Council:

Medical Information:

Car Insurance:

Car Breakdown:

Notable Dates

January
1 New Year's Holiday (UK & Republic of Ireland)
2 Holiday (Scotland)

February
14 Ash Wednesday
14 St. Valentine's Day
16 Chinese New Year

March
1 St. David's Day (Wales)
11 Mothering Sunday (UK)
17 St. Patrick's Day (Ireland)
19 St. Patrick's Day Holiday (Ireland)
25 Daylight Saving Begins
30 Good Friday (UK)
31 Passover (Pesach)

April
1 Easter Sunday
2 Easter Monday (UK & Republic of Ireland)
23 St. George's Day (England)

May
7 May Day Holiday (UK & Republic of Ireland)
28 Spring Holiday (UK)

June
17 Father's Day
21 Longest Day

July
12 Holiday (Northern Ireland)

August
6 Holiday (Scotland & Republic of Ireland)
27 Late Summer Holiday (UK)

Notable Dates

September
10 Rosh Hashanah (Jewish New Year)
11 Al Hijra
19 Yom Kippur (Day of Atonement)
21 The United Nations International Day of Peace

October
28 Daylight Saving Ends
29 Holiday (Republic of Ireland)
31 Halloween

November
5 Guy Fawkes Night
7 Diwali
11 Remembrance Sunday
30 St. Andrew's Day (Scotland)

December
21 Shortest Day
25 Christmas Day
26 Boxing Day
26 St. Stephen's Day (Republic of Ireland)
31 New Year's Eve

2017 Calendar

	JANUARY	FEBRUARY	MARCH	APRIL
Monday	30 2 9 16 23	6 13 20 27	6 13 20 27	3 10 17 24
Tuesday	31 3 10 17 24	7 14 21 28	7 14 21 28	4 11 18 25
Wednesday	4 11 18 25	1 8 15 22	1 8 15 22 29	5 12 19 26
Thursday	5 12 19 26	2 9 16 23	2 9 16 23 30	6 13 20 27
Friday	6 13 20 27	3 10 17 24	3 10 17 24 31	7 14 21 28
Saturday	7 14 21 28	4 11 18 25	4 11 18 25	1 8 15 22 29
Sunday	1 8 15 22 29	5 12 19 26	5 12 19 26	2 9 16 23 30

	MAY	JUNE	JULY	AUGUST
Monday	1 8 15 22 29	5 12 19 26	31 3 10 17 24	7 14 21 28
Tuesday	2 9 16 23 30	6 13 20 27	4 11 18 25	1 8 15 22 29
Wednesday	3 10 17 24 31	7 14 21 28	5 12 19 26	2 9 16 23 30
Thursday	4 11 18 25	1 8 15 22 29	6 13 20 27	3 10 17 24 31
Friday	5 12 19 26	2 9 16 23 30	7 14 21 28	4 11 18 25
Saturday	6 13 20 27	3 10 17 24	1 8 15 22 29	5 12 19 26
Sunday	7 14 21 28	4 11 18 25	2 9 16 23 30	6 13 20 27

	SEPTEMBER	OCTOBER	NOVEMBER	DECEMBER
Monday	4 11 18 25	30 2 9 16 23	6 13 20 27	4 11 18 25
Tuesday	5 12 19 26	31 3 10 17 24	7 14 21 28	5 12 19 26
Wednesday	6 13 20 27	4 11 18 25	1 8 15 22 29	6 13 20 27
Thursday	7 14 21 28	5 12 19 26	2 9 16 23 30	7 14 21 28
Friday	1 8 15 22 29	6 13 20 27	3 10 17 24	1 8 15 22 29
Saturday	2 9 16 23 30	7 14 21 28	4 11 18 25	2 9 16 23 30
Sunday	3 10 17 24	1 8 15 22 29	5 12 19 26	3 10 17 24 31

2019 Calendar

	JANUARY	FEBRUARY	MARCH	APRIL
Monday	7 14 21 28	4 11 18 25	4 11 18 25	1 8 15 22 29
Tuesday	1 8 15 22 29	5 12 19 26	5 12 19 26	2 9 16 23 30
Wednesday	2 9 16 23 30	6 13 20 27	6 13 20 27	3 10 17 24
Thursday	3 10 17 24 31	7 14 21 28	7 14 21 28	4 11 18 25
Friday	4 11 18 25	1 8 15 22	1 8 15 22 29	5 12 19 26
Saturday	5 12 19 26	2 9 16 23	2 9 16 23 30	6 13 20 27
Sunday	6 13 20 27	3 10 17 24	3 10 17 24 31	7 14 21 28

	MAY	JUNE	JULY	AUGUST
Monday	6 13 20 27	3 10 17 24	1 8 15 22 29	5 12 19 26
Tuesday	7 14 21 28	4 11 18 25	2 9 16 23 30	6 13 20 27
Wednesday	1 8 15 22 29	5 12 19 26	3 10 17 24 31	7 14 21 28
Thursday	2 9 16 23 30	6 13 20 27	4 11 18 25	1 8 15 22 29
Friday	3 10 17 24 31	7 14 21 28	5 12 19 26	2 9 16 23 30
Saturday	4 11 18 25	1 8 15 22 29	6 13 20 27	3 10 17 24 31
Sunday	5 12 19 26	2 9 16 23 30	7 14 21 28	4 11 18 25

	SEPTEMBER	OCTOBER	NOVEMBER	DECEMBER
Monday	30 2 9 16 23	7 14 21 28	4 11 18 25	30 2 9 16 23
Tuesday	3 10 17 24	1 8 15 22 29	5 12 19 26	31 3 10 17 24
Wednesday	4 11 18 25	2 9 16 23 30	6 13 20 27	4 11 18 25
Thursday	5 12 19 26	3 10 17 24 31	7 14 21 28	5 12 19 26
Friday	6 13 20 27	4 11 18 25	1 8 15 22 29	6 13 20 27
Saturday	7 14 21 28	5 12 19 26	2 9 16 23 30	7 14 21 28
Sunday	1 8 15 22 29	6 13 20 27	3 10 17 24	1 8 15 22 29

2018 Calendar

JANUARY

Monday	1	8	15	22	29
Tuesday	2	9	16	23	30
Wednesday	3	10	17	24	31
Thursday	4	11	18	25	
Friday	5	12	19	26	
Saturday	6	13	20	27	
Sunday	7	14	21	28	

FEBRUARY

Monday		5	12	19	26
Tuesday		6	13	20	27
Wednesday		7	14	21	28
Thursday	1	8	15	22	
Friday	2	9	16	23	
Saturday	3	10	17	24	
Sunday	4	11	18	25	

MARCH

Monday		5	12	19	26
Tuesday		6	13	20	27
Wednesday		7	14	21	28
Thursday	1	8	15	22	29
Friday	2	9	16	23	30
Saturday	3	10	17	24	31
Sunday	4	11	18	25	

APRIL

Monday	30	2	9	16	23
Tuesday		3	10	17	24
Wednesday		4	11	18	25
Thursday		5	12	19	26
Friday		6	13	20	27
Saturday		7	14	21	28
Sunday	1	8	15	22	29

MAY

Monday		7	14	21	28
Tuesday	1	8	15	22	29
Wednesday	2	9	16	23	30
Thursday	3	10	17	24	31
Friday	4	11	18	25	
Saturday	5	12	19	26	
Sunday	6	13	20	27	

JUNE

Monday		4	11	18	25
Tuesday		5	12	19	26
Wednesday		6	13	20	27
Thursday		7	14	21	28
Friday	1	8	15	22	29
Saturday	2	9	16	23	30
Sunday	3	10	17	24	

JULY

Monday	30	2	9	16	23
Tuesday	31	3	10	17	24
Wednesday		4	11	18	25
Thursday		5	12	19	26
Friday		6	13	20	27
Saturday		7	14	21	28
Sunday	1	8	15	22	29

AUGUST

Monday		6	13	20	27
Tuesday		7	14	21	28
Wednesday	1	8	15	22	29
Thursday	2	9	16	23	30
Friday	3	10	17	24	31
Saturday	4	11	18	25	
Sunday	5	12	19	26	

SEPTEMBER

Monday		3	10	17	24
Tuesday		4	11	18	25
Wednesday		5	12	19	26
Thursday		6	13	20	27
Friday		7	14	21	28
Saturday	1	8	15	22	29
Sunday	2	9	16	23	30

OCTOBER

Monday	1	8	15	22	29
Tuesday	2	9	16	23	30
Wednesday	3	10	17	24	31
Thursday	4	11	18	25	
Friday	5	12	19	26	
Saturday	6	13	20	27	
Sunday	7	14	21	28	

NOVEMBER

Monday		5	12	19	26
Tuesday		6	13	20	27
Wednesday		7	14	21	28
Thursday	1	8	15	22	29
Friday	2	9	16	23	30
Saturday	3	10	17	24	
Sunday	4	11	18	25	

DECEMBER

Monday	31	3	10	17	24
Tuesday		4	11	18	25
Wednesday		5	12	19	26
Thursday		6	13	20	27
Friday		7	14	21	28
Saturday	1	8	15	22	29
Sunday	2	9	16	23	30

January

Monday
1

New Year's Holiday (UK & Republic of Ireland)

Tuesday
2

Holiday (Scotland)

Wednesday
3

Thursday
4

Friday
5

Saturday
6

Sunday
7

January

January

Monday
8

Tuesday
9

Wednesday
10

Thursday
11

Friday
12

Saturday
13

Sunday
14

January

Monday
15

Tuesday
16

Wednesday
17

Thursday
18

Friday
19

Saturday
20

Sunday
21

January

Monday
22

Tuesday
23

Wednesday
24

Thursday
25

Friday
26

Saturday
27

Sunday
28

Monday
29

Tuesday
30

Wednesday
31

Thursday
1

Friday
2

Saturday
3

Sunday
4

February

Monday
5

Tuesday
6

Wednesday
7

Thursday
8

Friday
9

Saturday
10

Sunday
11

February

February

Monday
12

Tuesday
13

Wednesday
14

Ash Wednesday / St. Valentine's Day

Thursday
15

Friday
16

Chinese New Year

Saturday
17

Sunday
18

February

Monday
19

Tuesday
20

Wednesday
21

Thursday
22

Friday
23

Saturday
24

Sunday
25

Feb/March

Monday
26

Tuesday
27

Wednesday
28

Thursday
1

St. David's Day (Wales)

Friday
2

Saturday
3

Sunday
4

March

Monday
5

Tuesday
6

Wednesday
7

Thursday
8

Friday
9

Saturday
10

Sunday
11

Mothering Sunday (UK)

March

Monday
12

Tuesday
13

Wednesday
14

Thursday
15

Friday
16

Saturday
17

St. Patrick's Day (Ireland)

Sunday
18

March

March

Monday
19

St. Patrick's Day Holiday (Ireland)

Tuesday
20

Wednesday
21

Thursday
22

Friday
23

Saturday
24

Sunday
25

Daylight Saving Begins

Mar/Apr

Monday
26

Tuesday
27

Wednesday
28

Thursday
29

Friday
30

Good Friday (UK)

Saturday
31

Passover (Pesach)

Sunday
1

Easter Sunday

April

Monday
2

Easter Monday (UK & Republic of Ireland)

Tuesday
3

Wednesday
4

Thursday
5

Friday
6

Saturday
7

Sunday
8

April

April

Monday
9

Tuesday
10

Wednesday
11

Thursday
12

Friday
13

Saturday
14

Sunday
15

April

Monday
16

Tuesday
17

Wednesday
18

Thursday
19

Friday
20

Saturday
21

Sunday
22

April

Monday
23

St. George's Day (England)

Tuesday
24

Wednesday
25

Thursday
26

Friday
27

Saturday
28

Sunday
29

Monday
30

Tuesday
1

Wednesday
2

Thursday
3

Friday
4

Saturday
5

Sunday
6

May

Monday
7

May Day Holiday (UK & Republic of Ireland)

Tuesday
8

Wednesday
9

Thursday
10

Friday
11

Saturday
12

Sunday
13

May

May

Monday
14

Tuesday
15

Wednesday
16

Thursday
17

Friday
18

Saturday
19

Sunday
20

May

Monday
21

Tuesday
22

Wednesday
23

Thursday
24

Friday
25

Saturday
26

Sunday
27

May/Jun

Monday
28

Spring Holiday (UK)

Tuesday
29

Wednesday
30

Thursday
31

Friday
1

Saturday
2

Sunday
3

June

Monday
4

Tuesday
5

Wednesday
6

Thursday
7

Friday
8

Saturday
9

Sunday
10

June

Monday
11

Tuesday
12

Wednesday
13

Thursday
14

Friday
15

Saturday
16

Sunday
17

Father's Day

June

June

Monday
18

Tuesday
19

Wednesday
20

Thursday
21

Longest Day

Friday
22

Saturday
23

Sunday
24

Monday
25

Tuesday
26

Wednesday
27

Thursday
28

Friday
29

Saturday
30

Sunday
1

July

Monday
2

Tuesday
3

Wednesday
4

Thursday
5

Friday
6

Saturday
7

Sunday
8

July

July

Monday
9

Tuesday
10

Wednesday
11

Thursday
12

Holiday (Northern Ireland)

Friday
13

Saturday
14

Sunday
15

July

Monday
16

Tuesday
17

Wednesday
18

Thursday
19

Friday
20

Saturday
21

Sunday
22

July

Monday
23

Tuesday
24

Wednesday
25

Thursday
26

Friday
27

Saturday
28

Sunday
29

Jul/Aug

Monday
30

Tuesday
31

Wednesday
1

Thursday
2

Friday
3

Saturday
4

Sunday
5

August

Monday
6

Holiday (Scotland & Republic of Ireland)

Tuesday
7

Wednesday
8

Thursday
9

Friday
10

Saturday
11

Sunday
12

August

August

Monday
13

Tuesday
14

Wednesday
15

Thursday
16

Friday
17

Saturday
18

Sunday
19

August

Monday
20

Tuesday
21

Wednesday
22

Thursday
23

Friday
24

Saturday
25

Sunday
26

Aug/Sep

Monday
27

Late Summer Holiday (UK)

Tuesday
28

Wednesday
29

Thursday
30

Friday
31

Saturday
1

Sunday
2

September

Monday
3

Tuesday
4

Wednesday
5

Thursday
6

Friday
7

Saturday
8

Sunday
9

September

Monday
10

Rosh Hashanah (Jewish New Year)

Tuesday
11

Al Hijra

Wednesday
12

Thursday
13

Friday
14

Saturday
15

Sunday
16

September

September

Monday
17

Tuesday
18

Wednesday
19

Yom Kippur (Day of Atonement)

Thursday
20

Friday
21

The United Nations International Day of Peace

Saturday
22

Sunday
23

September

Monday
24

Tuesday
25

Wednesday
26

Thursday
27

Friday
28

Saturday
29

Sunday
30

October

Monday
1

Tuesday
2

Wednesday
3

Thursday
4

Friday
5

Saturday
6

Sunday
7

October

October

Monday
8

Tuesday
9

Wednesday
10

Thursday
11

Friday
12

Saturday
13

Sunday
14

October

Monday
15

Tuesday
16

Wednesday
17

Thursday
18

Friday
19

Saturday
20

Sunday
21

October

Monday
22

Tuesday
23

Wednesday
24

Thursday
25

Friday
26

Saturday
27

Sunday
28

Daylight Saving Ends

Monday
29

Holiday (Republic of Ireland)

Tuesday
30

Wednesday
31

Halloween

Thursday
1

Friday
2

Saturday
3

Sunday
4

November

Monday
5

Guy Fawkes Night

Tuesday
6

Wednesday
7

Diwali

Thursday
8

Friday
9

Saturday
10

Sunday
11

Remembrance Sunday

November

November

Monday
12

Tuesday
13

Wednesday
14

Thursday
15

Friday
16

Saturday
17

Sunday
18

November

Monday
19

Tuesday
20

Wednesday
21

Thursday
22

Friday
23

Saturday
24

Sunday
25

Nov/Dec

Monday
26

Tuesday
27

Wednesday
28

Thursday
29

Friday
30

St. Andrew's Day (Scotland)

Saturday
1

Sunday
2

December

Monday
3

Tuesday
4

Wednesday
5

Thursday
6

Friday
7

Saturday
8

Sunday
9

December

Monday
10

Tuesday
11

Wednesday
12

Thursday
13

Friday
14

Saturday
15

Sunday
16

December

December

Monday
17

Tuesday
18

Wednesday
19

Thursday
20

Friday
21

Shortest Day

Saturday
22

Sunday
23

December

Monday
24

Tuesday
25

Christmas Day

Wednesday
26

Boxing Day / St. Stephen's Day (Republic of Ireland)

Thursday
27

Friday
28

Saturday
29

Sunday
30

Dec18/Jan19

Monday
31

New Year's Eve

Tuesday
1

Wednesday
2

Thursday
3

Friday
4

Saturday
5

Sunday
6

January 2019

Monday
7

Tuesday
8

Wednesday
9

Thursday
10

Friday
11

Saturday
12

Sunday
13

Important dates

Important dates

Address & telephone

Name:

Address:

Postcode:

Telephone:

Work:

Mobile:

Fax:

E-mail:

Name:

Address:

Postcode:

Telephone:

Work:

Mobile:

Fax:

E-mail:

Address & telephone

Name:

Address:

Postcode:

Telephone:

Work:

Mobile:

Fax:

E-mail:

Name:

Address:

Postcode:

Telephone:

Work:

Mobile:

Fax:

E-mail:

Address & telephone

Name:

Address:

Postcode:

Telephone:

Work:

Mobile:

Fax:

E-mail:

Name:

Address:

Postcode:

Telephone:

Work:

Mobile:

Fax:

E-mail:

Address & telephone

Name:

Address:

Postcode:

Telephone:

Work:

Mobile:

Fax:

E-mail:

Name:

Address:

Postcode:

Telephone:

Work:

Mobile:

Fax:

E-mail:

Address & telephone

Name:

Address:

Postcode:

Telephone:

Work:

Mobile:

Fax:

E-mail:

Name:

Address:

Postcode:

Telephone:

Work:

Mobile:

Fax:

E-mail:

Address & telephone

Name:

Address:

Postcode:

Telephone:

Work:

Mobile:

Fax:

E-mail:

Name:

Address:

Postcode:

Telephone:

Work:

Mobile:

Fax:

E-mail:

Notes

Notes

Notes

Notes

Notes

Notes

Published and Printed by Danilo Promotions Limited,
Unit 3, The io Centre, Lea Road,
Waltham Abbey, EN9 1AS. Printed in South Korea.

Contact Danilo for a full listing of our complete
range of Calendars, Diaries and Greetings Cards
or find us on the Internet at:
www.danilo.com or email us at: sales@danilo.com

[f] /DaniloCalendarsUK   [t] @CalendarsUK